Becoming Jewish

Amy N Kaplan

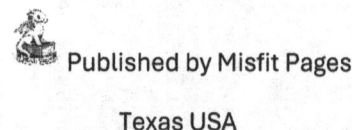 Published by Misfit Pages

Texas USA

On the World Wide Web at www.misfitpages.com

First Published 2024

ISBN: 978-1-962613-16-3 (First Edition)
ISBN: 978-1-962613-15-6 (Digital Version)

This book is a memoir. It depicts actual events in the life of the author as truthfully as recollection permits. Occasionally, dialogue consistent with the character or nature of the person speaking has been supplemented. All persons within are actual individuals; there are no composite characters. The names of some individuals have been changed to respect their privacy.

DEDICATION

To Rabbi Gaylia and Rabbi Charlie. Thank you for seeing me.
Your support let me find myself. I will forever be grateful.

INTRODUCTION

When I was going through the conversion process, my Rabbi told me to write a paragraph or two about my experience. I sat down at my computer and wrote nine pages before I had even realized it!

I never set out to write a book about my spiritual journey. However, the more I reflected on my life experiences, the more I realized how profoundly my quest for meaning shaped who I am. This book is not meant to be a definitive guide or manifesto. Rather, it is a personal account of the winding path that led me to find my true religious identity. I hope that by sharing my story, others may feel a sense of connection or inspiration. Whether you are on a similar journey, content where you are, or simply open to learning about different faith traditions, thank you for letting me share a piece of my heart with you.

PART 1

MY ENCOUNTERS WITH JEWISH PEOPLE

The first time I remember meeting someone who was Jewish was in the early 70s. I was probably about 6 or 7 years old. My dad had brought me to work with him at Frank's Pizza (they made the first frozen pizza for sale in grocery stores) and a man came in to see him. His name was Mr. Cohen. It was a weird interaction for me. Mr. Cohen asked me if I liked bagels and I said yes, even though I'd never had one before. He went out to his car and came back with a package of garlic bagels for me. (Still my favorite flavor) Mr. Cohen and dad talked for a bit and after he left my dad asked me what I thought about him. When I told him I thought he was nice he made some comment that I remember as being "even though he's Jewish." I had no idea what this meant. I saw him a couple of times after that (when dad brought me to work with him) and each time he gave me a package of garlic bagels. My childhood brain began associating bagels with Jewish people... much like it associated Italian people with pizza at the time.

We moved from Chicago to Erie in 1976 and my parents found a young girl to babysit us. I don't remember her name, but my parents liked her because she would babysit on Christmas and Easter because "she was Jewish, and those holidays don't mean anything to her." This was when I learned that being Jewish was a religion and began to understand that not everyone has the same relationship with God.

When I turned 11 my parents decided I needed to babysit other people's children. We had new neighbors who had just had a baby. Noah and Emma. Noah was a lawyer and Emma was a teacher. I babysat for them every Friday, and their house was always dark... only candles. I remember asking Noah why his calendar was different than mine and that's when he told me they were Jewish. Dad's only comment on the subject was along the lines of, "of course he's Jewish, he's a lawyer." I then thought that all lawyers were Jewish... my parents laughed but didn't correct this.

In 1979 my parents sent me to a private school where I met Olivia. At this school you didn't bring your lunch, the school prepared lunch and each grade (18 kids per grade) sat down and ate together. The headmaster would say a prayer before we were allowed to eat. At our table there was a second prayer said by Olivia. She didn't always eat the same food that we did. (Jane didn't either, but she was diabetic.) This was when I first heard the word Kosher. No one explained it to me, I just took it to mean there were foods you couldn't eat. I assumed all Jewish people were Kosher. While at the private school, we did a unit on food and nutrition for science class. Each kid had to bring in a food from home and explain it. Olivia brought in matzah. I thought it was a stale cracker. She said they used it instead of bread sometimes.

It wasn't until I divorced my first husband that I met

someone else who I knew was Jewish... my lawyer, Oliver. Dad said, "you need a good Jew lawyer." Turns out, he wasn't really a good lawyer and I had to fire him.

Then my brother began dating Isabella. My parents were civil to her and her mother but talked behind their backs in a condescending way. I didn't understand why they were so hostile... I still don't understand why. Isabella is intelligent, well spoken, funny... I liked her. I didn't see how religion had anything to do with whether or not you could like someone. Talks with Sophia (Isabella's mom) were insightful and enlightening. I found out that I could ask her anything and she didn't laugh at me for not understanding something.

I divorced my second husband and moved back to the United States (from Australia). After a year of finding myself and settling in I decided to start dating. This is how I met Herb, the love of my life. He stated from the start that he was Jewish. I honestly didn't care what his religion was. We had been going out for a few months when he asked me if I would go to a Friday service with him. That service was a turning point for me.

PART 2

MY RELIGIOUS UPBRINGING AND EARLY UNDERSTANDING

For as long as I can remember, my mom baked a birthday cake for Jesus on Christmas day. She said it was why we gave each other gifts. That made zero sense to me... and why the heck was Santa involved?

We went to church every Sunday until we moved to Erie Pennsylvania. I loved going to church. All my friends were there! It was called New Hope Community Church. I was in the children's choir. I got to wear a dress and wear fancy shoes... and I got to play with friends I didn't always see at school. At that time in my life church was a social event that occasionally had a few religious lessons thrown in.

When I was 6 years old my great grandmother gave me a children's bible for Easter. It was a big hardcover book with illustrations. She told me to read it aloud to her... I thought she was just testing me to see if I could read, so I needed to prove to her that I could! I started reading and had so many questions! I remember my parents laughing because I had questions and my great grandmother starting an argument... I was told to leave the room. (I took my book with me and read it.)

When I was 7 years old my friend Karen was outside in front of her house in a "wedding dress" and her whole family was taking photos. I asked mom why Karen was getting married and when she stopped laughing, she told me it was her first communion. (Our dictionary was no help here.) I wanted to know when

I'd get mine so I could wear a dress like that, and she said I couldn't because we weren't Catholic. (Again, the dictionary didn't help me.)

It was at this point that I found out I was neither Catholic nor Jewish. What religion were we? My great grandmother said she was Lutheran. My great aunt said she was Catholic. My father said he was Baptist. My grandmother said she was Presbyterian. My grandfather said, "I don't go to church anymore." Mom said, "You know what religion I am; we go to New Hope." I was so confused.

Aunt Mia took me to church with her on a Wednesday once when I was 7 or 8. A Wednesday!!! People did this? Great Grandma stayed at home... this was weird because they went everywhere together. (I now know it was because Great Grandma refused to set food in a Catholic church.) I remember a lot of standing, sitting and kneeling. They didn't speak a lot of English... and I had no idea what language it was at the time. (I now know it was Latin and we were at a Catholic church.)

It's now 1976 and we've moved to Erie. Mom said we had to start going back to church and she found one for us. My brother and I had to sit with her and dad instead of immediately running off to Sunday school. Then the minister called all of the children to come up to the front of the church. We had to sit up there on the floor while he talked to us. Then we were allowed to leave to go to Sunday school. Hooray, playtime! Because I was "new" I was peppered with questions I couldn't answer or didn't understand. I hated this. I never went back. I would sit with my parents and ignore whatever was being said by the minister. Apparently, dad wasn't keen on it either because we only went for a month or so before never going back.

It is now the summer of 1981 and we've moved back to Chicago and are living with my grandparents. I had to be enrolled in high school but there had been too many knifings at the public school for my liking. I convinced my parents to send me to one of the Catholic high schools. (Oddly enough, all my childhood girlfriends were going to the Catholic high schools instead of the public school.) None of the schools would admit me because we weren't Catholic. St. Cecilia's finally admitted me after they learned that mom's dad was Catholic.

This is the period of my life where I learned to dislike nuns. It is also where I learned the most about religion. My favorite joke became: What's black and white and red all over and can't fit through a doorway? A nun with a spear through her head. (I still giggle at this joke.)

My religion teacher, Sister Rose, was a sweet little woman who would answer any questions I had... no matter what they were. I drew a deeper understanding of what it was to be Catholic and knew that it wasn't anything like what I believed. I knew, from the classes with her, that I firmly disbelieved that Mary was a virgin when Jesus was born. I was certain that Joseph was the father of Jesus and all these people who believed otherwise were delusional.

My English teacher, Sister Alberta, was horrid. On my first day of school, she tried to show the class that a non-Catholic student doesn't know anything by asking me to write antidisestablishmentarianism on the board. When I spelled it correctly, she was angry and asked me what it meant. My understanding of the word, at that time, was vague so I told her all I remembered was that it had to do with the separation of church and state. She was livid. She never told me what the correct definition was. From that day on I was picked on continually. I was told I was going to hell, where I belonged, because I was not Catholic.

In 1982, before my freshman year of high school was over, we moved to Gallipolis Ohio. Once again, mom tried to find a church for us. We wound up in a Methodist church. I found the whole service to be odd. The minister spent most of the time yelling at everyone. He found many reasons why we would all go to hell, but only one way to go to heaven... being saved. What the heck was that? My friends at school told me being saved was when you knew that Jesus was the son of God and he died on the cross for you. Okay. So, was knowing this the same as knowing that 2+2=4? You're told it and you know it? How on earth can this be something that is celebrated as a big deal? Aren't you told this in Sunday school every year at Easter? Were you not paying attention? Being saved was, in my opinion at the time, stupid.

When I was 16, I went to church with a friend... he was Baptist. Not only did the minister yell at us about hell, but he also deliberately picked out me and my family and said we were paving the way for others to go to hell. You see, my dad owned a video rental business. Apparently, any movie with a rating other than G was evil. I ended up walking out of the service... after telling him I'd save his seat in hell.

I didn't go back to church until I was nearly 18.

PART 3

MY SEARCH FOR GOD

Most of my friends talked about religion. Well, they actually talked about Jesus more than anything. They talked about praying to Jesus, being saved by Jesus... it was all about Jesus! I felt that this wasn't right, at least not for me, so I decided to learn as much as I could about religion to make an informed decision.

I started by reading the children's Bible my great grandmother gave me. Then I read the Bible I got in Sunday school at New Hope community Church. Next, I read the Bible I had from St. Cecilia's High School. Wait a minute... the stories were similar, but not the same. If they're all the Bible, shouldn't they have been the same? I mean, I get the children's one being different as the language needed to fit the audience. But the messages were different. I gathered every Bible in the house and compared them. (One was in German; I have no idea what it said.)

I sought out the Priest at the local Catholic church and peppered him with questions he couldn't (or wouldn't) answer. Our next-door neighbor was the minister at the Methodist church... so I asked him the same questions I asked the priest. I was not getting answers to my questions, and I was learning that I didn't fit in to their belief systems.

I began going to church, on my own. I went to all the churches in the little town. I was trying to find God. I was trying to find where I belonged in all of this and who else had the same belief systems as me.

What did I believe? What didn't I believe? How did we get here? These were difficult questions. I began reading mythology... Norse, Greek, Roman, Egyptian. I understood why those cultures had so many gods... they were trying to answer questions like I was.

I knew there was a God. I believed that all of us were his children, so that made Jesus his son. I did not believe that Mary was a virgin (using today's understanding of the word) when Jesus was born. I knew that if Jesus had actually existed, he was the biological son of Mary and Joseph.

I knew that all those people praying to Mary and Jesus were wrong. The first commandment said that we would have no other gods. The second commandment said we wouldn't worship graven images. Good grief... they all pray to Jesus to save them... or Mary to help them. They bow down and pray before the cross, or an image of Jesus. What the actual heck?!! I KNEW this was wrong.

In college I met my first husband. He took me to church with his family after we were married, and it was a frightening experience. It was a tiny, Free Will Baptist church... and women had to wear a skirt or a dress; no pants allowed for women. The minister started the service and people would just get up and start "testifying" and referring to each other as "brother" or "sister" while proclaiming their love of Jesus. One woman just started to sing. Another began to cry because her sister "didn't know Jesus." I just sat there, confused. They played "find the Bible verse" game in the middle of the service... whoever found the verse first just stands up and begins shouting the verse. (so odd) And then, in some strange unspoken way, all the men went up to the front of the church and knelt in front of a tiny railing. Each one raised one arm toward the ceiling, bowed their head, and began to pray OUT LOUD. They were not all saying the same thing... each was praying something personal to Jesus, not God, as loud and obnoxiously as possible. A woman fainted. Someone else began to sing.

I was terrified that someone was going to begin to speak in tongues or they would bring out snakes... or both! Just as quickly as it started, it stopped. They all went back to their seats as if nothing had happened. The sermon began and it was the usual fire and brimstone you're all going to hell yelling-type speech. Frankly, I was no longer listening; I was just people watching at this point. I don't want to be yelled at about God, it's pointless. Next up was the "come up to the front of the church if the lord Jesus has called to you" nonsense. First off, he wasn't a lord. Second, you either believed it when it was taught to you, or you don't... it isn't an epiphany. Stupid. More tears and crying... singing and praying. Then someone said my name... what the heck? They wanted me to "testify" about my love of Jesus. No thank you. I'm just observing, not participating.

It is at this point that I decided that most religions seemed pretty stupid, and most people had no idea what they were talking about. I had read several versions of the Bible at this point and, thinking logically, could not see where they were coming up with their statements. My favorite questions to ask were:

1. And where does it say that Mary and Joseph were married but never had sex? (This invoked shock because I was saying two married adults might engage in this behavior.)
2. I don't recall reading the part where Joseph told Mary to "get out" when she said she was pregnant. Can you show me that passage?
3. Where, exactly, does it say that being gay is a sin? If we were all created in his image, and we are all "perfect" in his eyes, then a person's sexuality is beautiful to God, no matter what it is.
4. Please show me where the passage is that tells us it's now okay to pray to someone other than God... you know, like Jesus, because he isn't a god.

5. Why are some religions not allowed to talk directly to God? Why does there need to be a go-between?

My new sister-in-law was a Jehovah's Witness. She scared the heck out of the rest of the family... so I liked her immediately! I was curious about her religion because it wasn't something I had ever encountered before. She invited me to her house on the days she had religious instruction so that I could ask questions. I went twice... I'm not sure why I went the second time. I knew it was wrong about 15 minutes into the first visit. No wonder the family was scared. This seemed like a scary cult.

I had nearly given up on my faith at this point. Or maybe it was just that I couldn't find anyone who believed what I did?

In 1990 we found out we were expecting our first child. Our families were really excited... I was terrified. We were on a military base, and it was during Operation Desert Storm. Skylar's birth was a horror story... when I came to in the recovery room all I wanted to do was hold my baby. As soon as I held her in my arms and looked into her eyes, I knew she was a miracle from God. I also knew that I was never doing that again... my dreams of having four children were over.

My family needed us to christen Skylar. My husband's family said that you don't christen babies... you get saved. I said she could do both and arranged to have my daughter christened on Easter Sunday in the church I went to as a child... New Hope. The arguments were intense. I was having her christened to appease my family.

When Skylar was 9 months old God decided that I needed another child, and I became pregnant again. In 1992 my son, Edward was born. His birth was quick, easy and relatively painless... another miracle from God.

Did I mention the Mormons? While my first husband and I were living on the military base, a group of Mormons had been going door to door. This was a HUGE deal! No one could figure out how they got on the base. Frankly, I just wanted to see a copy of their Bible to compare it to my collection. Anyway, they eventually found their way to my door. I told them I wasn't going to let them in but would be interested in a copy of their Bible to study. They declined to give one to me, so I asked them to leave. I thought that would be the end of it.

A day or two later I was at McDonald's (in the little town near the base) with my one year old daughter. We were eating French fries and giggling when the same Mormons who had come to my home sat down next to me and my child. Skylar was sitting across from me in the booth... I became instantly terrified for her safety!

They said they had been waiting for an opportunity to speak to me again. I asked, "So you've been following me?" They answered that the Lord just wanted them to talk to me about the Kingdom of Heaven, so they had been watching me for a bit. Not wanting to scare my child, I began gathering what was left of our lunch while continuing to smile at my daughter. My mind was racing. This wasn't a religion I was interested in knowing ANYTHING about. I told the two young men that I had to change my daughter's diaper and would they please move. They did and I ran out to my car with my daughter, barely buckled her in her car seat and raced back to the base. I let the guards at the gate know what had happened. It turns out that the two young men were in the car behind me... they followed me back to the base! (I don't think it went well for them. No one ever saw them on the base again.)

So, Mormons were now not anyone I wanted to talk to – EVER! A religion that lets you think it's okay to stalk a young woman and a baby is not okay.

In early 1993, we bought a house in a little neighborhood behind a church, and I began taking the children every Sunday. My husband refused to attend. The congregation was welcoming, but it just wasn't "right." I felt like baby bear. I wanted my children to learn about God while they were young, but I needed to find someplace where I fit in. My search for a religious home began again.

When Edward was a year old, my family began asking in earnest when we were having him christened. The arguments started and I, once again, appeased my family by having my son christened at New Hope on Easter Sunday.

After Edward was christened, I had a sort of epiphany. None of these churches were "right" for me, but they all had one thing in common... they all believed in God.

My marriage was falling apart. My husband was having multiple affairs and the only thing we could effectively communicate about was arguing over religion. I convinced my husband to take a few days off work so that we could go and visit his family. We went to church with his parents and when the minister called people up to the front who had been moved by Jesus my husband got up and, with tears in his eyes went to the front of the church. My mother-in-law told me Jesus had washed him of his sins and he was ready to start over in the eyes of the lord. I began to cry, thinking maybe our marriage had a chance. My father-in-law misunderstood what was going on and told everyone that Jesus had finally come into my heart, and I was saved. (Oh boy) I respected this man and was not about to make him look like a fool in front of his peers... so I rolled with it. What was the worst that could happen? Well... the entire congregation went to a nearby farm where my husband and I walked into a "pond" and were full immersion baptized together.

It must have worked because our marriage was back on track, I thought, and in 1994 we found out we were expecting our third child. Things went south fast. My husband's affairs hadn't stopped. The abuse got worse. The day he hit Edward, twice, I knew I had to get out. I filed for divorce just before Thanksgiving that year.

I found a different kind of church while going through my divorce... Unitarian Universalist. Most churches were not accepting of me, a pregnant woman with two small children going through a divorce, but this one was. The congregation was somewhat friendly, but odd. They welcomed questions and there wasn't any yelling during the service. Maybe this was the right church?

In 1995 my daughter, Veronica was born. With the help of the minister at my "new" church I composed a naming ceremony (aka christening) for my daughter. There was no mention of worshipping Jesus. There was merely a quiet thankfulness for my miracle, her name and the reasons for it, and choosing two "mentors" to help guide her on a spiritual journey during her lifetime.

The whole ceremony felt more mystical and spiritual than religious, and I was quite happy with it.

In 1996 I married my second husband and we moved to Australia in 1997 after a lengthy court battle with my first husband. Moving to Australia was one of the best things I ever did for myself and my children. It was a fresh start.

In 1998 my fourth child, Benjamin was born. He was a beautiful little miracle. I had accomplished two life goals: being the mother of four children and living in Australia. My faith was renewed. I had no idea that another religious argument was headed my way.

My new in-laws wanted their grandson christened in their church in their hometown. I agreed since I had had the first two christened for my family... why argue about the fourth being done for his? His mother arranged everything... we just had to arrive with the baby, or so I thought.

My second husband's family was Church of England... so, basically Catholic lite. We had to meet with the archbishop the day before the ceremony so he could ascertain that we believed the "correct things" before he would christen the baby. Queue argument! I read through all the papers his mother handed me. It was nonsense and I would not say I believed any of it. I was not about to be in a "house of God" and lie about my relationship with God! Moreover, I had no intention of promising to raise my son to believe this drivel.

We finally agreed to tell the archbishop that I was a non-practicing Unitarian Universalist and that my husband's beliefs and mine did not align. We further agreed that it was my wish to christen the child in my husband's faith and let my husband guide him religiously. (My second husband was a former altar boy who was forced to go to church until he left home. He never wanted to set foot in that church again but was doing this for his mother.)

So, I found another religion that wasn't right for me. <sigh> I was beginning to feel alone. I didn't feel that I "fit in" anywhere. I despaired that no one else felt the way I did.

I met many people from many regions and religions while living in Australia. I met Hindus, Muslims and Buddhists. All of the women I met were lovely... their religions were interesting, but I still had my "baby bear" moments where it just wasn't right.

I met Harper, who was more spiritual than religious. We got on like a house on fire! Our children were similar ages, we had a lot in common... maybe I was spiritual and not religious too? Harper invited me to accompany her on a retreat she was going to, and my second husband agreed to look after the kids for the weekend while I went away on a "girls" outing. I had no idea what to expect.

We arrived at the retreat (a two hour drive to the middle of nowhere) and everyone was open and welcoming. Maybe a bit too open and welcoming. People I had never met before were hugging and kissing me. I needed my personal space! We went to put our things away in one of the rooms... and I discovered that it was all bunkbeds... and everyone slept in the same two rooms. NO. Not comfortable. There was a really creepy guy hanging around asking me which bunk was mine... I pointed to one on the other side of the room.

The food was fantastic! It was the best part of the retreat. Do I remember what I ate? Nope. But I have no negative memories about it, so there's that.

During the day (and night) there were a lot of group "sessions" going on. I tried most of them. One of them talked about chakras and auras. Apparently, mine was a mess and the color was wrong. Another talked about the use of crystals and their energies. The one that freaked me out the most started off okay. It was more like group therapy... and then someone I didn't know came behind me and began to give me a backrub. NOPE. I was done. I decided something with less human contact would be better, so I tried one that had me walk around a circular maze-thing. It was supposed to connect you to the spirits and energies or something. I was such a nervous wreck by the time I did this, that I cried through the whole thing. (This was misinterpreted.)

I decided I wasn't spiritual. I just wanted to go home. I saw less of Harper after that, but I don't know if the retreat was the reason.

I learned that a lot of people didn't understand that Christianity was a generic term that encompassed all religions that believe Jesus was the son of God. Most did not understand that Catholics and Church of England were Christian. I honestly became tired of hearing, "Well, I'm a Christian and..." as an excuse for whatever loathsome behavior they were displaying or ridiculous argument they were making. For example: "Halloween and Trick-or Treating are all about devil worship because I'm a Christian." (Never mind that the boy scouts invented trick-or-treating.) Or, "Well, I'm a Christian and the Bible teaches us that abortion is the work of the devil." Really? Where's that passage? Then there was the "Being gay is a sin against God. It wasn't Adam and Steve. I know, because I'm a Christian."

I knew I wasn't Christian; at least not by any of their definitions. So, what on earth was I? Where did I belong?

Fast forward to a trip back to the United States so that my first three children could have visitation with their father. Veronica had made an accusation about her dad. The judge didn't care and ordered the visitation to proceed. I felt like a part of me had died... like I'd been gut-punched and had my heart ripped out of me. I had failed to protect my children from an abusive man. They were now in God's hands... and I needed him to protect them for me.

I went back to my parents' house and took a long shower. I prayed. I cried. I beseeched God to look over my children, keep them safe from harm. I was vulnerable. I was alone. I was afraid. I made no promises; I was honest with God. A rush of intense love and peace washed over me. I felt, rather than heard, God telling me that everything was going to be okay. As I stood there in the shower, I saw faeries/angels/spirits, whatever you want to call them, surround me and then they left. I knew they were going to watch over my babies for me. I was at peace. The turmoil in my heart had stopped.

My relationship with God was back on track. I knew what I believed, but I didn't know what that religion was.

In 2010 my second husband and I decided to divorce. The children and I moved back to the United States to start over... again.

I had come to terms with my past. I had found myself. I didn't feel the need to go from church to church in search of the "right one" since I had been to most of them in the area. I just wanted to be me and be with my kids.

In 2011 I met Herb. At my first visit to the Synagogue, I felt comfortable. I felt welcomed. No one asked me about my faith. The Rabbis wanted to know if I enjoyed the service. They wanted to know if I had any questions. Yes! I have lots of questions. Rabbi Ruth took me on a tour and showed me the Torah. She explained what it was and its significance. She told me about the "hats" and "scarves" that some of the congregants wore. She told me about the prayers and songs. Then she did something strange... she invited me back. She asked me if I'd like to come back. She asked me. No one had ever done that before.

I saw Herb in a new light. This was his heritage, his background, his people. I wanted to know more about Herb. I wanted to understand more about him... and this religion was interesting!

That night I could hear the songs and prayers in my mind as I went to sleep. The Mi Shebeirach comforted me that night. I had never heard that before, but I couldn't forget the words. They spoke to my soul.

We went to the Synagogue together again and I "knew" the songs. I "knew" the prayers. The words were foreign to my ears but not my heart. I wanted to know more. Rabbi Ruth told me about the Introduction to Judaism classes that were starting up. She said I was welcome to come to any of the classes or seminars they held.

I began attending the classes. My "baby bear" was beginning to say "just right" but I didn't understand why. Rabbi Ruth asked me, in class, why I was there. I told her there were two reasons why.

1. I wanted to learn more about the man I was dating and falling in love with. Learning about his faith, since it was foreign to me, was a good way to accomplish this.
2. I had been on a "spiritual journey" to find the right church since I was a teenager.

The Rabbi said to me, "What if the right church is a synagogue?" I laughed at her and said, you can't become Jewish, you're born that way. She smiled at me and said, "no."

PART 4

EPIPHANY

I took all the classes the synagogue offered... sometimes 2 or 3 times. I went to services. I asked questions. Herb and I got married. Baby bear was happy. I found my religious home... but now I was asked if I wanted to convert. Not yet. That's a huge step. It isn't just a religion. Converting changes everything, or so I thought.

In 2016 Herb and I moved to Texas. We started looking for a synagogue. The first one we went to was a beautiful building... the congregants and the Rabbi didn't speak a word to us. (Baby Bear said it was too big.) Nope. The second one felt more like a cult than a synagogue. They were in a basement on folding chairs. There wasn't a Rabbi. The congregants were creepy. (Baby bear said it was too small.) Nope. The third one was juuuuust right. (Baby Bear moment.) We met Rabbi Ethan. The prayers were the same, but different. The songs had the same words, but different melodies. The congregants were welcoming and friendly. Rabbi Ethan made me feel at home.

By this time, I had begun to amass a library of books on Judaism. I was watching videos, reading books and, when we could, we attended services. Anyone who asked me about my religion was told, "I'm Jewish."

I felt as if my heart and soul had always been Jewish... it just took a while for my brain to realize it. I had a meeting with Rabbi Ethan... I don't remember what it was supposed to be for... but it ended up with me telling him I was ready to convert. I had never said that aloud to anyone before. It was time. It was time to outwardly show what I had always been inside.

And then I got scared again. I hadn't even told Herb that I wanted to convert! Ethan didn't push. He gently suggested that I watch some videos with other congregants who were converting, and I did. My fear was beginning to go away. We started going to services again... when we could. We owned a retail store that was open 7 days a week and we were there every day. (This made going to services every Friday somewhat difficult.)

Time passed. We hired a few employees for our store and decided to make time to go back to the Synagogue. We had plans to go to services one Saturday in January. I had arranged for employees to be there so that Herb and I didn't have to. But something happened... I don't remember what it was... and we didn't go. I hate to say it, but I'm glad we didn't go.

The day we didn't go to services was January 15, 2022... the day a man took four of my friends hostage at our Synagogue. I cried. I yelled. I prayed. I finally understood. My fears were gone. I knew, on that day, that converting was the right thing to do and I couldn't do it soon enough.

I am Jewish. This is my heart, my soul, my faith, my people. In a previous lifetime I'm certain I was Jewish... my soul is at peace and happy there. This is who I am, and I am proud to proclaim it out loud.

PART 5

CONVERSION

The day for my conversion had come. Herb took the day off of work. I told our employees I would not be coming into the store that day... so please keep the emergencies to zero.

There were two other people converting with me that day, Sarah and Michael. Sarah brought her two young children with her (they were also "converting.") and Michael brought his wife, Joan. Two gentlemen from the Synagogue, Jacob and Frank, were there as witnesses.

We all met up at one of the larger Synagogues in the area. Everyone seemed to be nervous about the beit din... except for me. They were worried about what the Rabbis would ask them and whether or not they would give the correct answers. I wasn't worried at all. I wasn't nervous. I welcomed the discussion with the Rabbis. I was looking forward to it.

I was more nervous about the mikveh. I can talk all day long... but the mikveh??? This was an unknown and I didn't have someone I knew to be there with me for it.

I got to go first for the beit din. Hooray! I went in and was rather surprised to find out that Rabbi Ethan had shared what I wrote with the other Rabbis. (You've been reading the same thing.) Okay, no biggie.

They had questions for me. I answered all of them honestly. I filled in details that were purposely left out. I told them why I was there. I have no idea how long I was there. I could have talked to them longer. (I don't think I've ever met a stranger.)

In the end they asked me, "What name do you want to give yourself?" Now, don't laugh. I decided on Ziva Davida. Yes, I loved watching NCIS. I hadn't told my husband what name I was choosing beforehand.

When I came out, Sarah and Michael asked me how it went. They wanted to know why it took me so long. (It did? I had no idea.) I was peppered with questions. Then they asked me about the name I chose. I told everyone... Herb just said, "Of course." Jacob and Frank said, "NCIS!!"

Sarah and Michael had their turns with the beit din. They shared their new names with the group and the reasons for choosing them. Then we all walked over to the mikveh.

I was a nervous wreck. This is the part I was unprepared for. I got to go first again. It wasn't as bad as I had it made out to be. Why on earth was I so worried??

Afterwards Sarah, Michael and I all got to hold the Torah. We had our photos taken with Rabbi Ethan. It was done. I was officially Jewish.

Rabbi Ethan said he'd like the three of us to come to services together so that he could formally "introduce" us to the congregation. We came up with a date that worked for all of us. It was set. Cool!

Then Rabbi Ethan said he'd like us to read what we had written about our conversion process to the congregation. It was at this point that he turned to me and said, "But not you. You are not reading all nine pages."

Sarah and Michael couldn't believe I'd written so much. Michael said he wrote a paragraph. Sarah said she wrote two. They wondered how I could write so much!

The day came. Rabbi Ethan was actually going to let me have a microphone and speak to the congregation... the fool! I am dangerous with a microphone. I go off script. I don't want to give it back once I have it. I LOVE speaking to groups of people... especially with a microphone!

Herb was worried. He knew what I was like. We had "stop" signals rehearsed. If he gave the motion, I was to stop speaking. Now the Rabbi was worried. I wasn't. I was excited. I was ready. I had nothing planned. I was winging it!!

It all went okay. I only spoke for about 3 minutes. I had them engaged. I could have gone longer. But the Rabbi looked nervous. Herb was getting fidgety, and he looked like he was going to use the signal. I thanked everyone for listening and handed the microphone to Michael.

It was a lovely service. Everyone there was so welcoming and friendly. Rabbi Ethan has moved to a new congregation. (I miss him.) I still see Michael at the Synagogue every now and then.

I got a certificate. Proof that I'm Jewish. I haven't picked it up yet. I keep meaning to, but every time I'm there, I forget. I think it's because I don't need proof. I am still me, just clearer.

The end, NOT!

POSTSCRIPT

In these pages, you've journeyed through the corridors of my life, glimpsed the highs and lows, and shared in the moments that shaped who I am. As we reach the end, I want to pull back the curtain a bit more. My name is Amy N Kaplan, the storyteller behind the words you've just traversed. Born in Chicago, every sentence penned is a brushstroke painting the canvas of my existence.

Family, my anchor through life's tempests, has been a recurring theme. The laughter shared over boardgames, the warmth of a familial embrace, and the profound joy of watching my children grow have been the keystones of my journey. In the tapestry of my life, they are the vibrant threads that add color and depth to the narrative.

As a writer, I've explored myriad genres, each story a chapter in my creative evolution. From whimsical children's tales, inspired by bedtime stories told to my own little ones, to the intricate worlds of role-playing games, my pen has danced across genres. Each tale, whether fantasy or reality, holds a piece of my soul.

And so, here we are at the end of this memoir, a shared experience between you and me. I am grateful for your company through these pages, and I hope my stories have resonated with you. As we part ways, know that the final chapter of this memoir is not the end but a new beginning. More stories await, and I invite you to continue this literary journey with me. Thank you for sharing this chapter of my life; may our paths cross again in the realms of imagination and beyond.

ABOUT THE AUTHOR

Welcome, dear reader, to the ever-expanding universe of Amy N. Kaplan, a prolific storyteller whose pen knows no bounds. Born in Chicago, Amy's journey has woven through diverse landscapes, both geographical and literary, shaping the vivid narratives that grace these pages.

Amy's storytelling repertoire has blossomed since our last encounter. In addition to enchanting children's tales like "Free Range Pigs" and "Free Range Bears," she invites you to explore new whimsical realms in "Free Range Goats" and "Nigel Needs a Home." These recent additions are a testament to her boundless creativity and commitment to capturing hearts across genres.

Venture further into the labyrinth of Amy's imagination with her debut romance novel, "Whispers of the Heart," where Daphne perseveres to finally find true love on her poignant, emotionally resonant journey of self-discovery. For fantasy enthusiasts, "Carnival of Shadows" awaits as a journalist races to uncover the sinister conspiracy behind the mysterious Carnival of Shadows before the murderous ringmaster and his circus claim more innocent lives in the small town of Ravensbrook.

Amy's storytelling prowess extends beyond fiction. In her memoir-style book, " With Ink-Stained Fingers and a Heart Brimming with Stories – Words" she bares her soul, inviting readers into the recesses of her memories, hopes, and dreams. Here, authenticity reigns, creating a unique bond between author and reader.

Family, always at the heart of Amy's tales, remains a guiding force. Her five children and two grandchildren continue to inspire narratives that celebrate the richness of familial bonds, creating stories that resonate across generations.

As you embark on this literary odyssey, know that Amy N. Kaplan is not just an author; she is your guide through worlds both familiar and fantastical. Whether you're here for heartwarming children's stories, passionate romances, immersive fantasy, or introspective memoirs, Amy invites you to explore the myriad facets of her storytelling tapestry.

So, dear reader, let the journey continue. Immerse yourself in the magic that is Amy N. Kaplan's latest collection, and may these pages be a source of joy, reflection, and discovery.

http://www.amynkaplan.com

OTHER BOOKS BY AMY N KAPLAN

Free Range Pigs: An Interactive Adventure Story about Three Little Pigs

Free Range Bears: An Interactive Adventure Story about Three Bears

Chronicles of Adventure: The Ultimate RPG Player's Companion

Chronicles of Adventure: The Ultimate RPG Game Master's Companion

Chronicles of Adventure: The Ultimate RPG Campaign Builder

Free Range RPG Player Journal

Free Range RPG GM Journal

Free Range RPG Campaign Builder

With Ink-Stained Fingers and a Heart Brimming with Stories – Words

WATCH FOR THESE EXCITING NEW TITLES

Free Range Goats: An Interactive Adventure Story about Ten Little Goats

Free Range Wolves: An Interactive Adventure Story about Three Wolves

Chronicles of Adventure: The Ultimate RPG Campaign Creator Guidebook

Carnival of Shadows

Nigel Needs A Home